PLANETS, STARS & GALAXIES

A VOYAGE OF DISCOVERY INTO THE MYSTERIES OF SPACE

Written by David Orme
Illustrated by Andrew Midgley

Collins Educational

An imprint of HarperCollinsPublishers

Looking into Space

Do you ever look up into the night sky at the stars?
Have you ever looked at the Moon through binoculars or a telescope? Have you wondered what it would be like to travel through space and visit other planets?

The planet we live on is part of the *solar system*. Including the Earth, the system has nine planets, and many smaller objects such as comets and asteroids. Most of the planets have moons. All of these – planets, moons, asteroids, comets – travel round the most important object in the solar system, the Sun.

The Sun is a star like every star visible in the sky. Other stars may have solar systems of their own, although their planets are too far away to see, even with powerful telescopes. Although Earth is the only planet with life in *our* solar system, there may be living things on other planets in orbit around other suns.

Solar System Countdown

9
Pluto's the lonely one,
Peering out into darkness
Like a lost dog.

8
Neptune swims through
The dark oceans
Like a giant sea monster.

7
Uranus is a big bouncy baby,
Waiting 84 years for his birthday.

6
Saturn smiles wickedly,
Flashing a wedding ring.

5
Giant Jupiter wants to be important,
But we know he has a big red spot
On his bottom.

4
Mars is red as rusty swords.

3
Earth's a bubble of life –
Mind you don't pop it.

2
Venus is a shy beauty.
She hides her face
Even from her friends.

1
Mercury's a sunbather.
He's got the best place on the beach.

0
The Sun – Fire!

How were the Sun and planets formed?

Some scientists think that the Sun and planets in our solar system were formed at the same time, when an enormous cloud of slowly cooling gases and dust was pulled together by its own gravity. The centre of this cloud formed the Sun, and what was left over made the planets.

3

Earth

I am the Earth.
Once, forest covered my face
Like a green beard,
And great animals hunted in it.
But now men come with sharp razors
To scrape my tender skin,
Leaving nothing but cuts and sores
and stubble.
Soon I will be barefaced and bald,
And the hot sun will burn me.
I'll never get used to it,
Even if it is
The latest fashion.

Zzzzxxx finds time to visit Big Ben during his whistle-stop tour of Planet Three.

4

The Earth

An alien reports on Planet Three

This solar system has nine planets, but only one of them has life on it. We have observed this planet very closely, and found it is a very strange place!

There are many different sorts of plants and animals, as there are on our world. The most intelligent animals are called 'Humans' and they call their planet Earth. It is surprising how much they have done, for they are very feeble creatures. They only have two of most things – two eyes, two ears, two arms and two legs. They can't run very fast, and have no shells on their bodies to protect them. They even have to wrap themselves in things called 'clothes' to keep themselves warm! They are very ugly creatures, with pink or brown skin and fur growing out of the tops of their heads.

Their planet is mainly sea. The land parts have beautiful forests, but the intelligent creatures are busy cutting them down. Perhaps they are not that intelligent after all!

They have already started to travel in space, and have landed on their moon. One day they will arrive on our planet. I hope they are friendly!

Signed **Zzzzxxx**

Zzzzxxx
Chief Explorer

EARTH FILE

Distance from the Sun:
150 million kilometres.

•

Diameter:
13,756 kilometres.

•

Average temperature:
22 degrees celsius.

•

Atmosphere: nitrogen
(about 78%), oxygen
(about 20%) with carbon
dioxide, and other trace
gases.

•

Highest mountain:
Everest (8,848 metres).

•

Number of moons:
1 (The Moon).

•

Length of day:
24 hours.

•

Length of year:
365 days.

The Moon

The Moon is our nearest neighbour in space. It is a satellite of the Earth. It travels round the Earth in the same way that the Earth travels round the Sun.

The Moon is a completely dead world, with no atmosphere. Its surface is covered with mountains and craters, and dark, flatter areas called seas (although there is no water). The craters were caused by meteorites hitting the Moon. Because there is no air or water on the Moon, the craters have not been eroded.

The Moon does not have any light of its own. It shines by reflecting light from the Sun. When the Moon comes between the Sun and the Earth it cannot be seen, because no light falls on the part facing the Earth. This is called a 'new Moon'. As the Moon moves round the Earth, more and more of the part illuminated by the Sun is visible to us.

The Moon always shows the same side to the Earth. The other side has been photographed by spaceships.

6

A Conversation with the Man in the Moon

Dear Man in the Moon,
Aren't you lonely, on your cold, dead world?

I am never lonely.
I am far too busy peeping through windows,
Tangling myself in branches of winter trees,
Admiring myself in muddy ponds.

What are you thinking, Man in the Moon?

I am thinking about what you are doing
to my friend, the Earth.

What would make you happy, Man in the Moon?

When you see me smiling down at you
From behind the chimney pots,
Please,
Smile back.

Why does the Moon appear to change its shape?

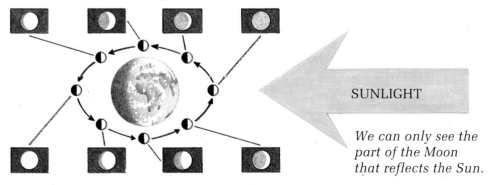

SUNLIGHT

We can only see the
part of the Moon
that reflects the Sun.

What Neil Armstrong *didn't* find on the Moon

"The Moon isn't made of cheese,
It's nothing but rocks and dust
Just like the Earth.
A pity really,
For I had brought my bread and butter
And was looking forward to a sandwich.

There isn't a Man in the Moon.
There's no-one here at all.
A pity really,
For I had made up a Moon language
And was looking forward to a chat.

There's nothing here at all.
I'm so disappointed.
I've decided to come home."

And as the Moon lander
Flashed upwards,
The Man in the Moon
Swept aside the dust,
Broke off a piece of really ripe cheese,
Munched it,
Licked his huge hairy lips,
And waved the Earthman
Goodbye.

MOON LANDING TIMECHART

July 1969 – Apollo 11
Neil Armstrong becomes the first man on the Moon.
First words on the Moon:
"It's one small step for man, one giant leap for mankind."

•

November 1969 –
Apollo 12
Second Moon landing.

•

February 1971 – Apollo 14
Third Moon landing.

•

July 1971 – Apollo 15
Fourth Moon landing.
Astronauts Scott and Irwin become the first people to drive on the Moon in their Moonbuggy.

•

April 1972 – Apollo 16
Fifth Moon landing.

•

December 1972 – Apollo 17
Sixth and last Moon landing.
Astronaut Eugene Cernan became the last man on the Moon – so far!

Satellites

Satellites are now very important to us. Some satellites broadcast television programmes down to Earth, while others are used for forecasting the weather. The world's first satellite was Sputnik I (see below) launched by the Russians in 1957. The photograph shows its various parts separated.

Space Junk

Fred's a solar junkman,
Cleaning up in space,
Solar cells and spacemen's boots,
Fred is on the case!

When junk from space comes raining down
The whole world cries for Fred,
"Now go and tidy up the stuff
That's falling on our heads!"
So Fred's ready with his junkship
When satellites wear out,
Space is always neat and tidy
When Junkman Fred's about!

Fred's a solar junkman,
Cleaning up in space,
Solar cells and spacemen's boots,
Fred is on the case!

Mercury and Venus

Mercury is the planet nearest the Sun, with Venus coming next. This means that both planets are too hot for life to exist. Mercury has very little atmosphere, but the atmosphere on Venus is extremely thick. Venus is a dangerous place. The temperatures are very high and the winds are terribly powerful. Venus landers have to be very strong to survive the great pressure of the atmosphere.

A Hot Day on Mercury

It's 100 degrees:
Hothead Sun
Hair all a sizzle,
Jumps out of bed.

It's 200 degrees:
A lovely day for a barbecue
Thinks the Sun,
Heating up the rocks
With a smile.

It's 300 degrees:
Mercury puts on his dark glasses,
Licks an ice cream made of lead,
And watches while it melts.

MERCURY FILE

Distance from the Sun:
58 million kilometres.

•

Diameter: 4,878 kilometres.

•

Average temperature:
Day –
350 degrees celsius.
Night –
-170 degrees celsius.

•

Atmosphere: Virtually none.

•

Number of moons: None.

•

Length of day: 59 Earth days.

•

Length of year: 88 Earth days.

Who were Mercury and Venus?

All the planets were named after ancient Greek or Roman gods. Mercury was the messenger of the gods. This was a good choice of name for a planet that speeds so quickly round the Sun! Venus was the beautiful goddess of love and fruitfulness. She is the only female god to have a planet named after her.

Here is an imaginary view of Venus through the porthole of a spaceship.

VENUS FILE

Distance from the Sun:
108 million kilometres.

•

Diameter: 12,104 kilometres.

•

Average temperature:
480 degrees celsius.

•

Atmosphere:
Very dense. It is mainly
carbon dioxide.

•

Number of moons: None.

•

Length of day: 243 Earth days.

•

Length of year: 227 Earth days.

Mercury

Venus

11

Mars

Mars is the fourth planet from the Sun, coming after the Earth, which is number three. Because Mars is further from the Sun than the Earth it is much colder. Its atmosphere is very thin indeed. Animal life is not possible on Mars because water could not exist on its surface. Mars is a cold, dry, dusty world. Huge sandstorms regularly cover the surface of the planet with red dust.

Photographs from probes that have landed on Mars show us that the surface is quite like the Moon. There are craters, mountain ridges and great dead volcanoes. The largest of these is *Olympus Mons*, a huge volcano three times higher than Mount Everest.

Close-up photographs show what look like dried-up river beds, which may mean that Mars once had a thicker atmosphere and water on its surface.

Mars

People have often wondered if there was life there. One day people from Earth will visit Mars. When they get there they will find that the gravity is less than on Earth, because Mars is a smaller planet.

Crewless probes called Viking 1 and Viking 2 (both launched in 1975) have landed on Mars and have sent back information and photographs about the surface. If there is life on Mars it would probably only be something simple like lichen or tiny germs, not the strange-looking Martians seen in science fiction films.

Canals on Mars?

When he looked through his telescope in 1877 the Italian astronomer Schiaparelli thought he could see channels or canals on Mars.

An Earthman sends a fax

The astronomers are right,
you know,
There are no canals on Mars;
There were a hundred years ago,
But now they've invented cars!

People thought that these might be the way that Martians travelled around their planet, or moved water around!

These days we have better telescopes and we can see that the canals do not exist. Nor do the Martians!

Jupiter and Saturn

Jupiter and Saturn are huge planets, mainly made of gas. Jupiter is the biggest planet in the solar system. The Earth could fit inside it one thousand times! Saturn is famous for its beautiful system of rings, made of pieces of ice and rock.

Jupiter and Saturn have many moons. The biggest moons of Jupiter are Io, Callisto, Europa and Ganymede. Ganymede is a huge moon, bigger than the planet Mercury. The biggest moons of Saturn are Mimas, Enceladus, Tethys, Dione, Rhea, Titan and Iaptus.

Jupiter

Ring Rise Over Mimas

From here, Saturn is so big
It's like a great, grey football
That's just about to hit you
on the nose.
When it decides not to
And stops and hangs there,
Wondering what to do next;
And the rings are like –
Like – hmm.

A hat brim with no hat,
A ring road dual
carriageway,
Cartoon people running
round and round
So fast they have turned into
a streak,
A hoop that someone has
thrown
Over the planet
To win
A star prize.

Who were Jupiter and Saturn?

Jupiter was the chief of all the Roman gods, the ruler of Heaven. Saturn was the father of Jupiter. He knew that one day one of his children would defeat him and become the greatest of the gods. He tried to prevent this by swallowing all his children as soon as they were born, but Jupiter was saved by his mother.

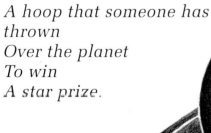

Saturn

SATURN FILE

Distance from the Sun:
1,400 million kilometres.

•

Diameter:
108,728 kilometres.

•

Average temperature:
-180 degrees celsius.

•

Atmosphere:
Very deep.
Mainly hydrogen.

•

Number of moons:
At least 17, plus the rings.

•

Length of day:
10.5 Earth hours.

•

Length of year:
Nearly 30 Earth years.

The Outer Planets: Uranus, Neptune and Pluto

The three outer planets are very cold indeed. Little heat from the Sun reaches them. Uranus and Neptune are large planets, made up of frozen gases with a rocky centre. Both planets have ring systems like Saturn and a number of moons. Pluto is a small, rocky and icy world. It has a moon, Charon, that is nearly half as big as itself. Some people call Pluto and Charon a double planet.

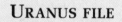

Neptune

Uranus

Pluto

URANUS FILE

Distance from the Sun:
2,870 million kilometres.

•

Diameter:
50,724 kilometres.

•

Average temperature:
-214 degrees celsius.

•

Atmosphere:
Hydrogen and helium.

•

Number of moons:
At least 15.

•

Length of day:
17 Earth hours.

•

Length of year:
84 Earth years.

NEPTUNE FILE

Distance from the Sun:
4,500 million kilometres.

•

Diameter:
50,538 kilometres.

•

Average temperature:
-220 degrees celsius.

•

Atmosphere:
Hydrogen and helium.

•

Number of moons:
At least 8. The biggest is called Triton.

•

Length of day:
19 Earth hours.

•

Length of year:
165 Earth years.

Not Many Rhymes for Pluto

I'm an oval orange alien
I live on Pluto
what a handsome guy am I,
I am so cute -O
nly little problem's
I'm a real tough brute -O
gre faced with size forty boots -O
vergrown head but my brain's minute -O
bedient to no-one, with power that's
absolute -O
ld as the planet and tough as a boot -O
come and pay a visit in your little space
suit -O
bey what I say
spend a day
on Pluto

PLUTO FILE

Distance from the Sun:
Varies. Nearest 4,425 million kilometres, furthest 7,375 million kilometres.

•

Diameter: 2,324 kilometres.
(Pluto is the smallest planet.)

•

Average temperature:
-230 degrees celsius.

•

Atmosphere:
Methane and nitrogen.

•

Number of moons: 1.

•

Length of day:
over 6 Earth days.

•

Length of year:
over 248 Earth years.

Pluto is usually the most distant planet from the Sun, until it comes inside the orbit of Neptune. It is then nearer to the Sun.

17

Asteroids

Between the orbits of Mars and Jupiter are found around 40,000 chunks of rock, from the size of a Moon down to small pebbles. These are called asteroids. Most of the asteroids of the solar system are found in this belt, although there are others elsewhere in the solar system. Some asteroids come close to the Earth. When an asteroid hits the Earth, it is called a meteorite. Luckily, most meteorites are very small.

Asteroids contain useful metals and other minerals. One day, space miners may be able to land on asteroids to extract the metals and minerals for use on Earth. Some scientists think that it will be possible to bring asteroids close to the Earth ready to be mined, by using giant sails in space! There is no wind in space, and these sails would be pushed along by sunlight.

SOLAR SYSTEM TIMES

September 5th, 2078

ASTEROID ARRIVES IN EARTH ORBIT

Early today a huge asteroid, measuring 25 kilometres in diameter, was parked in Earth Orbit. The asteroid, known as Lucky Strike 2, contains many valuable minerals. It has taken five years for the asteroid to reach Earth using giant solar sails. Chief miner Kelly Brown said that she was pleased that the giant asteroid had reached Earth at last, and she and her team were ready to start work.

Meteors, Meteorites, and Comets

Meteors are sometimes called *shooting stars*. If you are lucky, you may see the light of a meteor as it streaks across the sky. The light is made by the materials of the meteor burning up in the sky. Many millions of meteors reach the Earth every day.

Meteorites are larger than meteors. They may be tiny asteroids. Often they can reach the ground and larger ones will leave craters. In 1954 a meteorite crashed through the roof of a house in the USA, but no-one has ever been killed by a meteorite.

Comets orbit the Sun like the planets. They are made up of pieces of rock and ice surrounded by gases. When they pass by the Earth, we see them as very bright objects with long tails of shining gases. Halley's Comet comes close to the Earth every 76 years.

Meteorite – a riddle poem

Once
A gold meteorite landed in my garden.
I looked out of my window,
Saw
A flash, a tail of fireflies, then
Thwack!
It landed in the cabbages.
In the morning I looked for it,
Found it soggy and empty,
But I could still read
GOLDEN METEORITE
Light blue touch paper
And
Retire

What *really* landed in the cabbages? *Answer on page 32.*

The Sun

The Sun is a star, just like all the other stars in the sky. It looks much bigger, because it is much nearer to us! All the planets travel round the Sun. Without the Sun, there could be no life on Earth. The Sun gives us the light and heat that makes life possible.

The Sun is very big and very hot. On the outside of the Sun the temperature is about 5,500 degrees celsius, while in the middle it is fifteen million degrees!

Old ideas about the Sun

Before modern astronomy, people had unusual ideas about the Sun. Many thought it was a god and worshipped it. Ancient Greeks and Romans saw the Sun as a great golden chariot, pulled by horses across the sky. Native Americans from California believed that the Sun was the big chief. The Moon was his wife and the stars his children. Every day the stars would disappear very quickly when the Moon appeared, otherwise their father, the Sun, would eat them! Some native Australians believed that at the end of each day the Sun ran out of firewood to burn, and had to go into the underworld to get some more. This was why it went dark at night.

The Egyptians thought that their sun god Ra travelled across the sky in a boat. Every morning he had to defeat a ferocious dragon so that he could shine again.

Most early astronomers thought that the Sun travelled round the Earth. The famous sixteenth-century astronomer Copernicus said that the planets travelled around the Sun, but not everyone believed him!

Eclipses of the Sun

An eclipse happens when the Moon comes between the Earth and the Sun, blocking out some of the Sun's light. A total eclipse of the Sun happens when the whole of the Sun is covered by the Moon. When this happens it is possible to see the *corona* or 'atmosphere' of the Sun.

Total Eclipse of the Sun.

An Eclipse

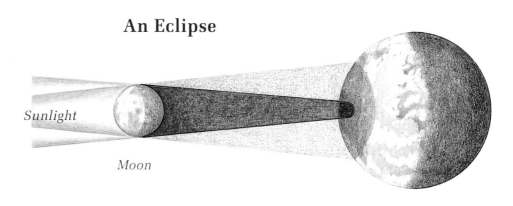

Sunlight

Moon

Earth

Hot Stuff

A raging fire is nothing like the Sun;
The whole Earth burning wouldn't be as bright.
The Sun's an engine, that will always run
Without a hitch, and give us heat and light.
We always grumble when there's cloud about,
And feel depressed. We do so love it when
We wake and find the Sun's already out,
Rain's gone, and summer days are here again!
So if you moan, when sun gets in your eyes,
Or when your body's turned a sunburn pink,
You'd best remember, if you're truly wise
To stop complaining, have a little think,
Just how it comes to be we're warm and fed,
and think of sunless planets, cold, and dead.

21

The Stars

The stars are suns. Some are smaller than our Sun, some are much bigger, but all of them are very far away. The light from our Sun takes just over eight minutes to reach the Earth. The light from the nearest star takes over four years to reach us. The light from more-distant stars can take hundreds of years to reach us.

Many stars have a partner. The stars are held together by gravity. These are called *binary* stars. Any planets of binary stars would have two suns!

Stars are not all the same. Some are hotter than others and they can be white, orange or red. Astronomers think that stars change as they get older. Originally the star forms when dust and gases come together. After many millions of years a star like our Sun runs out of the fuel that feeds it and it grows much bigger, turning into a red giant. After millions of years the red giant will shrink down into a white dwarf.

When these changes take place any planets will be destroyed. Luckily this will not happen to our Sun for millions of years!

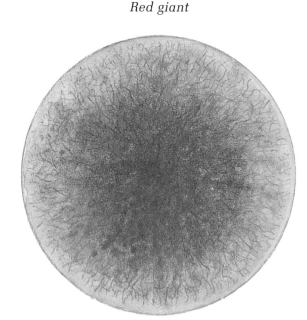

Red giant

White dwarf

22

Travelling to the Stars

Stars are so far away that a journey there would be impossible with the spacecraft we have now. It would take eighty thousand years for a rocket from Earth to reach the nearest star!

How can we reach the stars?

• A spaceship world

Families could live their lives on a spaceship. Eventually their great-great (and many more greats!) grandchildren would reach the stars. The ships would have to be a complete world in themselves, where food could be grown and water recycled.

• A long sleep

Some scientists think that in the future it might be possible to put people into a deep sleep that would last for centuries. When their spaceships reached the stars, automatic machinery would wake up the sleeping crew. Of course, when they arrive there might not be any planets suitable for living on. Perhaps they would have to go back to sleep and come all the way back!

• Travel much faster

Scientists believe that the speed of light is the fastest speed possible. Maybe one day ways will be found to make spacecraft travel faster than light, and people will be able to take their holidays on planets travelling round distant stars!

Star words

Can you guess these words? They all begin with *star*. Use your dictionary to help you.

1 Look intently at something.
2 The right-hand side of a boat.
3 Something used to make clothes stiffer.
4 Common, speckled bird.
5 Sea creature with five arms.
6 Someone who begins a race.
7 Very hungry.
8 Make someone jump!

Answers on page 32.

Constellations

The stars appear to group together in a series of patterns in the sky. These are known as constellations. On clear nights, many of these are easy to see.

Because the Earth moves round the Sun, the constellations appear to move around the sky. This means that not all the constellations can be seen all the time, and they will not always be in the same place. Some constellations can only be seen from the northern hemisphere, and some only from the south.

Here are some of the best-known constellations. Try and find them in the night sky.

Orion is named after a hunter in ancient legends. Look for his sword hanging down from his belt. In the sword you will be able to see a nebula. (Find out more about *nebulas* on page 28.)

Not far from Orion's left shoulder is *Taurus*. It is named after a bull, but it doesn't really look like one!

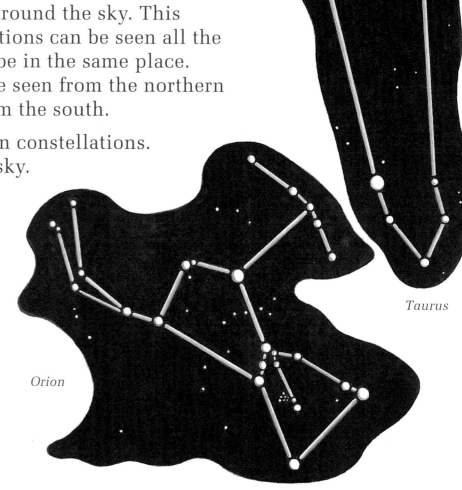

Taurus

Orion

24

Probably the best-known of all the constellations is the one known as the *plough,* the *great bear* or the *big dipper.* It really looks more like a saucepan! Astronomers call it *Ursa Major.* Nearby is *Ursa Minor* or the *little bear.* You can use these constellations to help you find the pole star. This star seems to be fixed in the sky, with all the other constellations moving around it.

One of the most famous constellations, seen only from the southern hemisphere, is the *Southern Cross.*

Cassiopeia is easy to spot, as it is shaped like the letter W.

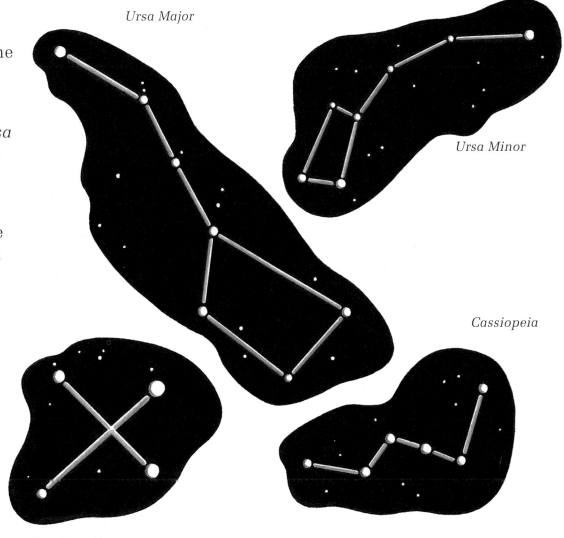

Ursa Major

Ursa Minor

Cassiopeia

Southern Cross

Galaxies

Our Sun is part of a huge collection of stars that make up our galaxy. There are around a hundred thousand million stars in the galaxy. Our galaxy is shaped like a spiral. At the centre stars are very close together. Our Sun is in one of the arms of the galaxy, half way between the centre and the edge. Light takes 100,000 years to travel from one side of the galaxy to another!

Our galaxy, sometimes, known as the Milky Way, is one very ordinary galaxy. In space there are many others, no-one knows yet how many. Many of the galaxies are spirals like the Milky Way, but some are elliptical galaxies (egg-shaped), with no 'arms'. Galaxies come in groups. Our own group has about thirty galaxies in it. Most of them are smaller than the Milky Way.

How to see what our galaxy looks like

I stir
My coffee cup,
And see, in its brown froth,
Spinning galaxies with bubbles
For stars.

The syllables in this cinquain poem form a sequence. Can you work it out? *Answer on page 32.*

How to spot a galaxy

During the late autumn and winter find *Cassiopeia*, the constellation shaped like a W. Below it you will see a square of stars – this is the constellation *Pegasus*. Between them you can see a smudgy patch. This is the biggest galaxy in our local group. It is sometimes called the *Andromeda Nebula* but it is not really a nebula at all. A better name is the *Great Spiral*. Astronomers call it *M31* – not a very exciting name!

Nebula

A nebula is a great cloud of gas in space. They may be the places where new stars are being created. To see a nebula find *Orion* (see Constellations, page 24). The nebula called M42 can be seen in Orion's sword.

Nova and Supernova

Stars sometimes flare up in a great explosion, then become fainter again. Astronomers think that these 'novae' happen in double star systems, when one star 'sucks' material from the other one, causing a great flare in space called a nova. (Two of them are called novae, not novas.)

When very large stars have used up all their hydrogen fuel they can collapse, and then explode. This huge

The Orion Nebula

explosion is called a supernova. After the explosion there is often a cloud of dust, with a small, very heavy star at the centre.

Pulsars

It is thought that the small, very heavy stars left after a supernova may spin round very fast. Radio astronomers can detect these because they send out a regular 'blip' as they spin, like the beam of light from a lighthouse only much faster.

Black holes

Sometimes stars become too heavy even for themselves! They keep on collapsing, getting smaller and smaller, until they create a black hole. Anything coming near a black hole would be sucked into it. Even light cannot escape from a black hole!

For a star or cluster of stars to make a black hole in space they have to shrink until they are made of material so heavy that a piece the size of a pin head would weigh millions of tonnes.

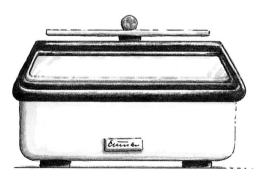

If the Earth shrank into a black hole, it would end up the size of a pea, but it would still weigh the same as the Earth does now!

What happens to things sucked into black holes?

No-one knows!

How did the Universe start?

Scientists think that the Universe started with a massive explosion 15,000 million years ago. We call this explosion The Big Bang. The Universe is still getting bigger and bigger. Astronomers know this because they can see distant galaxies moving away from us.

Black hole poem

"I've got you in my clutches," said the black hole to the light, "You'll never get away from me," he laughed, "Sweet dreams! Night Night."

Telescopes

Optical telescopes use lenses and mirrors to magnify objects in space. Large telescopes have cameras attached to them to take photographs in space. The problem with optical telescopes is that they cannot operate when the sky is covered with cloud.

The Mount Palomar Observatory which houses the Hale Optical Telescope

Radio telescopes

Light is only one of the 'messages' we receive from outer space. Many other rays come from space; radio waves, cosmic rays, ultra-violet and infra-red rays, microwaves and others. Telescopes have been built to detect all of these different rays. Radio telescopes pick up radio waves. Some of these come from the far edges of the universe.

The radio telescope in the picture above is the Lovell telescope at Jodrell Bank, in England. The biggest radio telescope is at Arecibo in Puerto Rico. This telescope has broadcast a message from Earth into outer space. So far, there has been no reply. One day, perhaps, we might hear a big hello from an alien civilisation far out in space!

The Hubble Space Telescope

The Hubble Space Telescope is able to look deep into space without the Earth's thick atmosphere getting in the way. The Hubble telescope was launched from the space shuttle in 1990. Unfortunately there was a problem with one of the mirrors and the pictures sent back to Earth were not as good as they should have been. A second shuttle mission corrected the mirror, and now the telescope is sending home wonderful pictures of objects in space.

Index

Answers

Page 19

A **firework** fell into the cabbages!

Page 23

1 stare
2 starboard
3 starch
4 starling
5 starfish
6 starter
7 starving
8 startle

Page 26

The syllables in the cinquain poem are arranged like this:

2

4

6

8

2